M000306244

THE BURDEN OF LIGHT

Poems by

Deena Metzger

OTHER WORKS BY DEENA METZGER

FICTION

A Rain of Night Birds
La Negra y Blanca
Feral
Doors: A Fiction for Jazz Horn
The Other Hand
What Dinah Thought
The Woman Who Slept With Men to Take the War Out of Them
Skin: Shadows/Silence

NON-FICTION

From Grief Into Vision: A Council

Entering the Ghost River: Meditations on
the Theory and Practice of Healing

Intimate Nature: The Bond Between Women and Animals
(with Brenda Peterson and Linda Hogan)

Writing For Your Life: A Guide and Companion to the Inner Worlds

Tree: Essays and Pieces

POETRY

Ruin and Beauty: New and Selected Poems
Looking for the Faces of God
A Sabbath Among the Ruins
The Axis Mundi Poems
Dark Milk

DRAMA

Dreams Against the State
Not As Sleepwalkers
Book of Hags

THE BURDEN OF LIGHT

Deena Metzger

Hand to Hand is a community based endeavor that supports independently published works and public events, free of the restrictions that arise from commercial and political concerns. It is a forum for artists who are in dynamic and reciprocal relationship with their communities for the sake of peacemaking, restoring culture and the planet. For further information regarding Hand to Hand please write to us at: P.O. Box 186, Topanga, CA, 90290, USA. Or visit us on the web at:

www.handtohandpublishing.com

Donations to organizations have been made to replenish the trees that were used to create the paper in this book. We also wish to acknowledge the RSF Social Finance AnJel Donor Advised Fund for their support.

"An Opening," given honorable mention, First *Topanga Messenger* Poetry Contest, July 2014.
"The Common Way," was published in *Askew* 2015.
"Our Radiant Lives" was published in *Dark Matter*: Women Witnessing, Issue 3.
"The Burden of Light," was published in *Topanga Messenger,* July 2017.
"The Sea Hemorrhages Oil Through Its Night," and "Early Morning Beauty Flees" appears in the Los Angeles poetry issue of *Pratik,* 2019.
"You Know It's All Going Down Now, Don't You?" is from *World on Fire*, a Poetry/Music Theater Piece conceived and performed by co-creator Naomi Newman.

The Burden of Light. Copyright © 2019 Deena Metzger
ISBN: 978-0-9983443-2-4

"Blue Doorway" Mandala, Book and Cover Design: Stephan David Hewitt
All Photographs by Deena Metzger
Cover Photo, "Sun Rising at Lough Crew, Ireland, Fall Equinox 2012"
Author Photo by Jay Roberts

All rights reserved. No part of this book may be used or reproduced in any manner whatsoever without written permission, except in the case of brief quotations embodied in critical articles and reviews. For information please contact the publisher at Hand to Hand, P.O. Box 186, Topanga, CA 90290.

Printed in the USA by Hand to Hand Publishing.
05 04 03 02 01

Acknowledgements

This book results from a most precious friendship and collaboration over the years with Stephan Hewitt, the publisher of Hand to Hand. It was his idea to use my photographs but more importantly, this book has become a work of art, through his eye, skill and heart. Please note, also his mandalas which introduce and close the book, taking us into the depths where the poems live.

I am so grateful to Stephan and Naomi Newman who insisted that the book come into the world. And also, of course, to Earth and the myriad beings from which all life emerges and on whose behalf these words were written.

For Naomi
Who loves the Earth so!

TABLE OF CONTENTS

PREFACE

I want you to read this entire book, cover to cover like a prayer for us, because it is a prayer, and it is like a mantra, because, as its planet-haunted and haunting author, Deena Metzger knows in her bones, it is maybe all we have, all we will — have. Because she is a seer. And poetry is her staff, as she crosses the land, a woman of a certain age, she knows that her voice and her calling is our deep red thread to follow in the dark ... to our own knowing, also.

> Once all co-existed: light, dark, wolves,
> trees and rain, the newly born and the dead.
> Now all of us in our separate graves.

She speaks to the Earth and to our terrors. She speaks to and of the animals. And she knows, and we must know that we come from a dire past.

> Sometimes the eucalyptus
> bleeds red sap to its roots.
> Maybe it remembers men
> hung from its branches.

She speaks with the vulnerability of being mere human, mere woman, speaking truths.

> I didn't know I would be lonely at this time in my life
> whether or not the creatures gather to receive a simple
> offering of seeds.

She speaks to the mountain lion:

> "Neighbor," I said in a whisper
> so as not to startle him.
> Or maybe I said, "Friend."

Deena Metzger is the sphinx who knows the answer to our direst questions, and yet she is living in the question. Are we?

I thought I could quote only a few of her words and began writing them down to share with you, but every poem has lines I want you to hear as I have been hearing them since I began reading this newest volume. I knew when I was a very young poet and read her words that she was a voice to learn from. Her "Burden of Light" breaks the heart while it teaches. My heart is broken along with hers for the life we have left. Yet her words are talismans to hold. I began to select lines and excerpts and verses at random, because I do not want to die, and yet....she shows me/us how to do so, eventually. All I could do was to read and re-read. I want to scatter her words like water over a drought. Like love over a torment like Abu Ghraib. Yes, this book comes to remind us as it must, and as we must remind one another, of "The Burden of Light."

There is a Chinese proverb I encountered once that speaks about how at birth a child is given a thin red thread that ties it to who she is meant to be with. These poems of Metzger's are such a thread. I feel we are meant to be with them until the end, and until the beginning.

Because... here is a poet who reminds us:

You must not turn your head away
in grief, and fail to see the wings...

margo berdeshevsky

http://margoberdeshevsky.com

THE BURDEN OF LIGHT

THE AFTERMATH

If in the aftermath of darkness
a sun falls on us
in its silver casing,
how will me meet
that blinding light?
I do not want
to love you so
to extinction,
but in the way
of the hearth fire,
the small candle,
and the lowly match.

THE COMMON WAY

Three hundred yards after the turn
onto the road, the words are "Gratitude" and
"Thank you," as the mountains loom up
on both sides of the road.
Soon the sycamore will appear
and other trees and plants so common,
I do not know their names.
I have been driving this road
for thirty-three years and
when I do not drive anymore,
I want to end here, where I have lived
so long I know the land but not
the houses that come and go,
to end here among the coyotes and the owls,
the mourning doves and the ravens,
where the road turns. The yellow sign that
purports to describe the road, is only
a sign, is not an augury. This path
does not require divination because
it is so simple. We leave and we come
home. We learn the way. We walk the path.
It happens again and again,
and then it won't. I live at the end
of the road. And so it shall be.

THE BURDEN OF LIGHT

The Butterfly, with the burden of light
on its back, weaves across the meadow
where the slightest green emerges
after four years of drought.
The sage has survived, although
it has been ash black for months.

It's a Monarch attaching
to the eucalyptus blossoms among the Bees.
Small brown leaves flutter down,
columns of broken wings in the wind.

The clouds gather again in faint promises.
We continue to water
what we can reach of the wild and feral,
returning some of what we have stolen.

We look to the North to redeem us.
The Polar Bear mother will not survive.
As we burn, her cub will drown.
Still, we pray that her grief
will rain down upon us this season.

RETURN AT THE TURN OF THE LABYRINTH

Sacred stones scattered in the fields
among the holy Cows and Bulls
grazing by the river Boyne.
Boann the goddess, running her blue waters
through the grasses toward the blessed wells.
The Milky Way and Taurus roaming the sky.

Earth is a mirror, the way the moon
follows the sun, longing for light.
And here come the clouds, writing
fate and messages in shapes and shadows.
Beauty rains down and rises up,
seeps into all the cracks of my broken heart.

When my friend was dying
her world view was reduced to a window.
It was sufficient for the miniaturist,
her careful, minute strokes
the equivalent of alpine flowers.
I don't know why
I am telling you this here,
but it matters. Death teaches us
how to see, but often it is too late.

I walk past the cemetery, down the narrow road
bordered with foxglove, and sweet blackberries,
and choose my medicine carefully,
walking into a circle of grasses,
forming a labyrinth bending in the wind.
From the center, we can see the sea
and the ring of mountains.

I have always known the Hag,
the circle, the council,
the cycle of day and years,

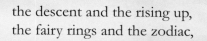

the descent and the rising up,
the fairy rings and the zodiac,

the places where death fades into birth,
where, as in this moment,
throwing the white bones,
remembering, begets the future.

I step out of the house.
Time to hit the road. Let's
meet what is coming
even if it requires
leaning on a walking stick.

The holy Cow, bovine river and stars
know the way. She presses forward,
chewing, chewing the sacred cud,
the eternal grasses rising from the bog.

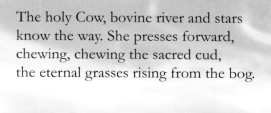

CALLED BY THE DEAD
Autumn Equinox at Loch Crew September 21, 2012

Called by the dead,
who had not expected
this resurrection,
I follow the light
into the dark chamber
where signs, carefully inscribed
on stone, were buried
with their bones.

Even if I return,
as they have,
neither you nor I
will remember.

Above the mounds,
the crows and ravens
wheel in windy knots,
landing in the oaks,
so that we think death
is in the trees, cawing.

But death
is living under our feet.
The dead hold us up.
Even the ancestors
whose names and lives
we have forgotten.

It takes a year, it's said,
for the bones to speak
their silent language,
arranging themselves
upon the altar,
or being exiled
to oblivion.

I have come here
to see my future;
the dissolution
that nourishes the living.
My body, your food
in a new form.
The circle of the earth
rounded out under our feet,
our dead burrowing beneath.

We descend and rise up.
The secret and ongoing communion.
The sun parts the clouds,
a procession of souls
longing for form,
sweeps across the mounds,
and enters the chamber.

In time,
you will take me
into your mouth.
It is unavoidable, this grace.

APART FROM BEAUTY

For Nora and Anne

I left you Beauty
and you diminished.
Was it, perhaps,
my distraction and preoccupation
with good deeds,
always on your behalf,
and the associated absence of my heart,
that allowed your territory to contract,
allowed the ever expanding

domination by my alien species,
blind to who you are,
to establish our domain
where your spirits had once thrived?

A simple walk among the trillium,
blue cohosh and trout lilies
arising in the moist and secret places
beneath the trees felled
by the terrible October cold snap,
returned me to the girl
who safely walked the neighborhood
each night, learning the way.

There are those
who meditate in caves for years
on behalf of the world.
If I walk silently,
in the remaining patches of creation,
without leaving a mark,
breathing and blessing,
might this give you heart
to become a tumbling vine,
the ivy of restoration,
making your way, tendril by tendril

over what we install,
thinking our own lives
might be separate from you,
not seeing our death
in the mirror of retreating waters?

I walk again
in the young ways I knew
when I was wiser
and had no ambition
but to learn the way of poetry
from the weeds and the wild grasses,
the sea pounding the shore,
the heartbeat
I let slam against me,
then continued on my way
in moonlight and shadow,
relentlessly thirsty for your light,
offering myself
to your tutelage.

I did not know
I must not leave you,
I did not know that thinking
I had learned what I needed
for my life, and stepping away,
erased everything.

Is it too late?
Am I too old?
Will we both go down together?

Oh, but the trillium,
is it a sign?
Can we bloom again
against all odds
of heat, storm and ice?

I will go out of my house,
open the gates to the wild,

call down the hunted Mountain Lions,
Wolves and Bears,
and yield my land
to those companions,
in your name.

NEIGHBOR

I was reviewing my life,
like an adolescent
imagining a future
when she will walk
in the dark moon shadows,
and speak to strangers
about the forbidden.

The girl I had been,
went on the land
at high noon,
turned to the four directions,
calling each by name.

I wanted a path to take me forward,
though I knew that the future
is only a reflection,
that all there is,
is what already has been.
Then, I saw movement
across the chaparral
among the oaks and boulders.

A young Mountain Lion came out
from the trees, turning his head
toward me. We stood eye to eye,
his tail flicking to every thought.

"Neighbor," I said in a whisper
so as not to startle him.
Or maybe I said, "Friend."

To end this way, at peace
with what is beyond me —
a child, walking
the neighborhood all night,
turning around the lighthouse,

and meeting the sun,
four-legged and wild near the finish.

Nothing else.

What was,
the next instant,
se fué.

LION

For Naba

There were others saved once.

I don't know about my people,
that is, the small family
that when shot, fell into the ditch
one upon the other,
for comfort on the other side.
Perhaps I passed by their mass grave
when I was on the road
driving to Treblinka or Auschwitz,
because I needed to know everything
to prepare for these last years.

There were others saved once.
What is the price you will pay?

Soon after we met,
you became a refugee.
I used that word, and exile,
and you refused to hear them.
You could only say,
"I want to go home."

Your son says, "Please do not come home;
you will be shot." He writes to us from France, saying
you are a difficult woman.
You will not cover your head.
Your arms are bare in the heat.
You will not forget you are a Professor,
you know biology.
You are stubborn, he says,
you will not forget your studies,
that you are an expert
on the science
of all forms of life.

In your dream, possibility depends
upon offering two chickens
and a gift to the beggar woman
at the corner. You have to telephone
Baghdad for the gift to be given
outside the green zone.

Now only poverty protects your house
with its broken windows,
all the glass on the photographs shattered
and the art collection covered in ash.
Sometimes, it seems,
you are too depressed even
to suicide in your daughter's home.
Against your will,
you apply for asylum.
It will drive you mad, you say.

The Koran lies in the yellow dust
of a bomb crater that now carries
its own radiant light; it will last
ten thousand years.
All Merciful.
All Compassionate One.

Yesterday, the Wolves attacked
little Lion Dog who had come
up the long hill as a friend,
and dared to eat their food.
Hearing the cries,
I threw myself upon their bodies
and she ran off,
but not without her wounds.
Another kind of salvation.

When we see into the future,
we will see Lion Dog

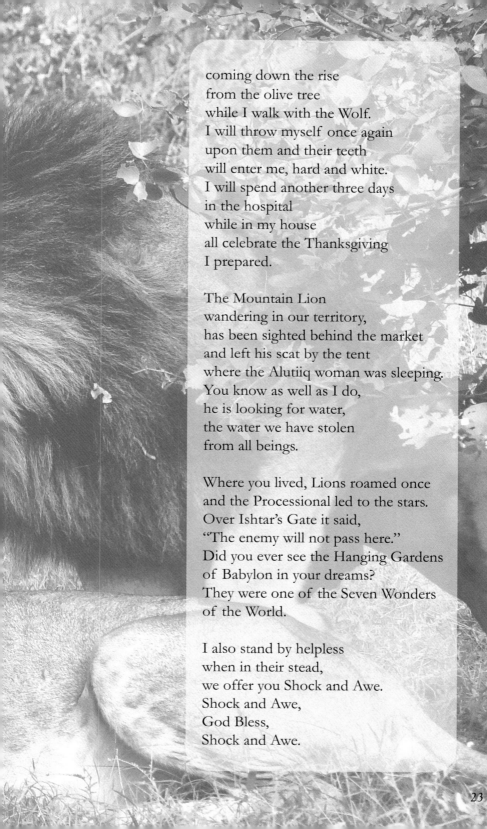

coming down the rise
from the olive tree
while I walk with the Wolf.
I will throw myself once again
upon them and their teeth
will enter me, hard and white.
I will spend another three days
in the hospital
while in my house
all celebrate the Thanksgiving
I prepared.

The Mountain Lion
wandering in our territory,
has been sighted behind the market
and left his scat by the tent
where the Alutiiq woman was sleeping.
You know as well as I do,
he is looking for water,
the water we have stolen
from all beings.

Where you lived, Lions roamed once
and the Processional led to the stars.
Over Ishtar's Gate it said,
"The enemy will not pass here."
Did you ever see the Hanging Gardens
of Babylon in your dreams?
They were one of the Seven Wonders
of the World.

I also stand by helpless
when in their stead,
we offer you Shock and Awe.
Shock and Awe,
God Bless,
Shock and Awe.

BRIDGING THE REALMS

A long limb extends from the elm across the secret garden to be lost in a flurry of rose bushes, honeysuckle and Rose of Sharon. A bridge from the outside entrance to the interior patio where the community gathers. Two Squirrels transit the limb, meeting in the center, then one chasing or courting the other. And so it has been for days, but until now I did not recognize that they are coupled, that this is their home parallel to mine.

They pause and stand, sentry-like, peering into the window where I am writing. I pause and peer back. These words do not matter to them as they stand in spring alert between curiosity and wariness. I didn't know I would be lonely at this time in my life whether or not the creatures gather to receive a simple offering of seeds.

(ANIMAL) TERROR

That (animal) terror
considered the worst
that *we* can experience,
must be within the animals now,
as they cannot escape us
anywhere on the earth.

We determine their lives.
We are their persistent and
ever present companions,
their stalkers, their hunters,
their wardens, their killers,
their common terrorists,
their Abu Ghraib.

THE SEA HEMORRHAGES OIL
THROUGH ITS NIGHT

Driving past cemeteries
we go down with our kin,
into the black seas
the Whales cannot breach.
I ask the dead to rise,
as the living are taking all life.
Perhaps the dead can return it,
bone, for white bone,
for white bone, for white bone, for white bone...

DEATH, BLACK AS A CROW

It could not bring me to believe in death.
Feathers so radiant with light
could only be the night sky,
could only be eternity.

A stream of blood from its yellow beak
drying on the pavement.
The roots of the tree
were not the right burial ground,
a neighbor's cat was wandering
up and down the entrance
to the *shul* among the olive trees,
and though the ravens had fed Elijah,
I could not bring the one,
who had received the gift of dark from Apollo,
to *Kol Nidre*, the Hebrew prayer for the dead.

We spoke, he and I, as I drove us home,
of what concerns all sentient beings,
of all the vehicles that kill.
This morning, I laid him on the hill

At the feet of Avalokitesvara
Infinite compassion.

I stroked his feathers. I wanted
the dark light on my hands.
I did not take a wing or a single feather
though I know the animals
will dismember him,
despite his shroud
of pine needles and tobacco.

Here is my prayer:
Do not forgive us our transgressions.
Let the black light
that surrounds you
meet the ancient fire
in the core of the earth,
for the marriage of prophecy
and possibility. Sunlight
inherent in your beak,
speak to us.

Death,
Be so tender with me
When you lay my body down.

EARLY MORNING BEAUTY FLEES

Gold at the edges of the eucalyptus vanishes
in the coming day and wind. Yeats understood:
terrible beauty emanates from the mind.
We walk the land. We tell the stories: visions
and death. Here the Wolves returned to the Earth
from which they leaped into life. Here they were
born and here they burrowed back. The grass ripples
and we offer ourselves, but briefly, to the day.

Light and dark vanish, but they return.
Then water vanishes; we cannot imagine it.
We still prefer our dry lives. Oceans rise up
but we cannot get to the heart
of the matter. The sky withholds itself
from our Midas touch. How quickly the golden light
escaping the bank of clouds, turns the leaves brown,
returns as fire. Once all co-existed: light, dark, Wolves,
trees and rain, the newly born and the dead.
Now all of us in our separate graves.

THE EARTHSEA MOTHER

In order to hold the EarthSea Mother
and her burning water,
I have to be in the water
and burn with her.
She cannot bear it
or escape it,
and neither can I.

There is no way to hold the Mother
without being inside the Mother,
holding her. And if
I can be filled with joy
when I am holding her,
the joy flows into her,
the way she flows into me.

The EarthSea Mother,
the burning waters,
I hold her and
I am immersed in her.
Joy flows as relentlessly
as fire. Joy flows.
Fire flows. We are one
And we are each other.

YOU DON'T HAVE TO
TURN YOUR HEAD

You don't have to turn your head,
birds of different species
will cross your vision
each moment and in each direction,
which is, as it was once,
and still is in this minute sanctuary
called the restoration of memory.

You must not turn your head away
in grief, and fail to see the wings,
and remember how it was,
and still is when you dare
to stand there, emboldened by the past
arising at the insistence of beginning.

A SILENCE THAT CALLS
WITHOUT A NAME

Preparing as for a long journey,
considering that I may not return,
recognizing the choice in this moment

to write *I* instead of *one,*
thus acknowledging that, finally,
I am speaking of my own life,
and not life in general,
which I cannot know
but from within myself.

Entering the field or habitat
of silence as a way
of freeing myself
from all that is not myself,
from all that is not
the way spirit knows me.

Here I am, I say
this morning, without knowing
whether these simple words
are also the sacred *hineni,*
while praying they are.

Silence calls and so I answer,
entering unknown territory,
to explore through grief
for my own life, suddenly shattered,
and my grief, and yours,
for the world, shattered,
splintered, crushed, smashed,
almost beyond recognition.

Story says that women of my age
retreated to the edge of the woods,
not out of despair or uselessness,
but to gather wisdom the way
women still gather the fallen wood
to build fires to provide
warmth and feed the ones they love.

Here are the woods.
Here are the fallen branches.
Here is history in the leaves and bones.
Here is one question to consider:
Will we die of old age and natural causes
or will we be hunted down?

I stand with the Wolves
when I ask this question.

YOU WANT TO KNOW

You want to know who or how I am,
want some poetic revelation, if not quite
the current story between my legs —
do I have a story at this age? —
then some other secret you will treasure
and assume we know each other well.

But is this body not the ravaged earth?
And if I tell you I am burning,
that I live the auto-da-fé each day,
don't you know that I
see the match you hold?

CRIME AND RETRIBUTION

For Tobi

A friend and colleague
dreams three words:
"Stop all poison."
But oil spills, fracking,
genetic modifications,
pesticide, nuclear waste
seep into the water table
which is, after all, our blood.

Also of our own making,
planes crash,
buses collide,
trains derail
and there is a plague
of maddened men
taking up automatic weapons
and killing, the way
we wipe out Ants.

Not to mention
the massacre of Wolves,
the mafia of poachers,
flying in to decimate tribes
of Elephants for the tusks
that promise longevity,
and great Whale singers
harpooned, their blood tide
tainting the poisoned seas.

My Native friend says
the Great Sea Mother
is angry, noting
fires and floods,
earthquakes, tornados,
hurricanes, tsunamis
and typhoons.

In desperation,
knowing there is
no solution,
Japan releases
a thousand tons
of contaminated water
into the sea.

A radioactive plume
makes its way east
to the US west coast,
seeping through
dark waters
into the living world.

Yet, at the same time,
I experience a radiant
outpouring of love.
One spiral
from another source
of light,
meets so many others
on this small planet.

We think this is
a potent remedy,
though a fierce medicine
and demanding regimen.

But we do not have
the courage
of belief,
we do not dare
the vortex of undoing
what must be undone
in order to heal.

YOU KNOW IT IS ALL GOING DOWN NOW, DON'T YOU?

You know it is all going down now, don't you?

Where shall we begin the rosary of grief?
With the Wolves they want to hunt from the sky?
When they disappear, so will the trees.
All beauty will go down in the bloody
grave of the natural world.

The Deer, denied her rightful death,
is sighted in the crosshairs of the rifle
and sinks to her knees
before the hunter trained in Vietnam
or Iraq. A drone above his head
seeks out his body heat
and puts an end to it.
He knew, didn't he,
what was coming?

On the ground, a robot moves,
unafraid, ahead of troops,
shooting straight at any movement.

In the short time before the enemies
have their own iron men,
we assume the drone
will not frag the officers,
or indulge friendly fire,
but you never know.

Every nightmare we have imagined
is being birthed now, all at once.
What had been written as a warning
has become strategies, tactics and plans.
I did not wish to live to see this day.

Radiation burns.
Oil burns.
Phosphorus burns.
The earth is burning.
Everything is set on fire.

Therefore, beat the man
almost to unconsciousness
then plunge his head in water,
until he prays to drown.

How many forms of torture
can you name
that are occurring now?

Your young child,
the innocent one,
a gun forced into her fists,
will do the same,
even to you.

Reb Nachman of Bratslov
speaks of the King who
refused the portion of grain
different from that
which would drive
all the people mad.

Though declining, he said,
"We will mark our foreheads,
and seeing each other,
we will know we are insane."

Know that we are mad
and live accordingly,
also seeking the hidden
passageways of beauty
that insist we leave
everything behind.

MEDICINE WAYS FOR THE
WORST OF TIMES

There is no way we can win against the elementals.
They will take us down by our own hands.
Uranium belongs to the realm of Oya. Everyone knows
    you don't mess with Oya.
Earthquake. Tornado. Lightning.
Storms of all sorts describe her even temperament.
The EarthSea Mother rises up, despite her pain.
There is no telling what will occur and no restraint. It is all
    herself.
She does not make those divisions we insist are there.

EarthSea Mother, Fukushima and the waters at the
    Columbia Gorge.
Fire next time? Burning waters. Warnings:
"If you eat a hundred pounds of fish from the Columbia
    River a year,
one pound every three or four days, the normal and sacred
    diet ...."
Cancer is one name for her rage.
There is nowhere we can go.
She is everywhere. Didn't you know?

The Spirits are sassy. That line in the water,
between Japan and the USA, isn't firm enough to stop her,
nor the legal border between Oregon and Washington.
And, temporarily, or forever, she is in this body. See?
If and when she rises and tries to rid herself of the fires ....
Beware.

Sometimes a cloud is just a cloud,
and sometimes it's the entire sky racking down endlessly.
Don't get lost in minutiae while the world is destructing.
Be aware that you are destroying your little life,

and also the ten gold finches on the arc of the metal chair,
and the hummingbird dipping

into the waters bubbling from the crown chakra
of Avalokitesvara, or Kwan Yin, or the Buddha fountain.

Another thing: let us not argue so that peace can descend.

The best medicine has not been invented yet,
but you know what it is and it takes you
completely by surprise. All the fevers,
tumors and agonies were created just for it to emerge.
How else will it get into the world?
Do you want to wait until you are struck down?
Or do you want to try to carry it on behalf
of what you love inconsolably — the Earth.

JUST IN

When I open the package
the Justin Boots announce
they are carcinogenic,
so I can die
with my boots on.

ELM

Between the end of the year
and the beginning,
when dying turns into birth,
the colors of the dawn
strike the old elm
without mercy.
The leaves continue to fall,
and its dark limbs
remain so murky despite
the momentary gold.

THE FOG CLOSES IN

The fog closes in tight.
All the gloomy Junes we've ever known
extend into October.
The ghosts come close,
the melting snows burrow
into the ground also seeking shelter.

My voice returns,
and my hopes rise
as I recognize it.
Whatever is to be said
begins with the Earth and weather,
even if I am in inadmissible despair.

And why language?
Without sentences, the Squirrels
do no harm to each other.
You think it is the thumb,
but I think words are
the core of our defeat,
though there is nothing
I would rather do
than shape words
to protect what lives.
We stood still while
the sheer white cloud filled the valley.
like a bandana, the man said,
like a lake, the woman answered.
A bandage, I thought, and above it
the dark hills, houses, electric lights
scattered like oaks or manzanita.
And above them, the moon

a crescent, a cup of fog
reversed, overflowing.

Sometimes the eucalyptus
bleeds red sap to its roots.
Maybe it remembers men
hung from its branches.

We stood and stared until
the earth vessel stopped filling,
the momentum of fog ceased.
Then we went inside.
Who wants to read?
One voice and then another.
Nothing spoken could have been anticipated.
Every word from the spilled bowl of sky
filled the wounded Earth,
a few wisps of cloud there,
here, a tourniquet.

THE ORCHARD IS FERAL

I've let the orchard go feral.
We offer it nothing but water,
and take nothing,
but leave it to the Bees
who sing among the blossoms,
and to the Squirrels who gather
the oranges and grapefruits
that fall and scatter.
The lemons and oranges
have mated on their own.
Maybe they will remain coupled,
or maybe the hybrids will sort themselves out,
returning to their original natures.

This time, the old elm is dying,
a very few branches have leaves.
There will be none next year
except for the sapling that is streaking
toward the sky. I sometimes think,
I will die with the elm, but wonder
if its progeny means a new birth for me.
It is, after all, from the old root.

Everything must have its way.
The oak that planted itself
created its own field of being,
so the others accommodate
to its shady dominance.
The creatures eat,
but they do not slaughter.
The old, old ways insist
that the animals can teach us
the difference between their natural order
and our domination.

The plumbago expands between
the eucalyptus trees that plant themselves,
increasingly at the border, providing
shelter for the Squirrels and a Thrasher,
occasional Quail and a flock of brown birds
who prefer to remain anonymous.

We are advised not to plant these trees
as they will burn hot and fast
when the great fires come. But
it is their will to abide here.
And who am I to deny them their homes?
They are no more alien than I
and also, at this time, they are
calling the cool winds to them,
the heat of the neighboring meadow
entirely dispelled by their fluttering arms.

And, you must understand that
we are in a conversation about
what it will take to call down the rain —
but only for the frogs, for the non-humans —
from this desert blue sky.

AN OPENING

An opening was promised for weeks,
encouraged by sunshine,
but nipped, so to speak
by the oddly cold nights,
until the heat struck suddenly
and the brush burst into ocher flame.
Everything went up in smoke,
the pesticides and chemicals
roaring into dark fire.
Then the acacia bud,
that had been waiting,
blossomed, yellow to yellow.
The delicate life,
and the terrible death,
meeting, it seems,
at last.

ATTACHMENT

What was the poem that slipped through my fingers
when I forgot that age is certain and the past
far longer than the future?
It was something about the way life clings to the body
as sky attaches to earth though also infinitely far away

That was it:

The way life clings to the body
as sky attaches to earth
though also
infinitely far away.

Cheyenne is home
hungry, distraught, confused
wishing to be outside
and inside at the same time,
with me and alone simultaneously.
The pleasure of his animal body
alongside me,
and the heartbreak,
his
and mine.

GRIEF, WHAT IS IT?

Solstice 2012

Grief! What is it?
Grief is:
Nothing can be done.
Do nothing then,
wisdom answers.

A calendar resets
the days of our lives
as if given another
chance to invite beauty
to rain down from the sky.

As I write this, the light
glazes the leaves
that seem to be holding on
between green and yellow.
What holds them to the branches
when others are on the muddy ground?

For three days, we followed
the dying years
across the Milky Way.
Who knows
what is at the end of the line
when nothing is done?
A flower emerges or falls,
each will occur in time.
Meanwhile, let's not
count our losses
or our gain.

GRIEF?

Grief?
What is it?
Simple.
Grief is.
Nothing can be done.
Grief is nothing can be done.

KILLJOY

When we look out at the mountains,
we think we are immortal,
then we see the peaks that have been sheared,
the walls and fences, lawns and roses
sustained by pesticide, replacing the sage,
where Bees once lived.

Anything can be destroyed by the human hand.
Sometimes a garden is an act against nature.
I bought an orchard and let it go feral,
but the Wolf is on a leash because
you will shoot her in the street and
sell her pelt to someone like me.

There was a poem about not telling the truth,
but it was disappeared.
The truth I refused was that I will die
sooner than expected and I will not be ready.
I will not have done what must be done.
Every day that I forget
is a crime against what must be said:
Evil is a plague designed as weapons of war.

What if in this life, I could save one creature
and its life force would multiply?
What if every bullet bounded back to its source?
Sometimes I believe
that if I could find the right prayer,
the river of blood would clear.
How many land mines and drones
must we nullify in order to walk
on the land again?

We tried to save one bull Elephant
who was seeding generations,
the hunter shot the Matriarch instead.
Why does killing pleasure you so?

Remember when invaders
came down from the North
with their weapons and Horses?
Now we are hunting the Horses.

You would like another ending to this poem,
I would like it if the world wasn't ending.

What else is there to say?

We are either killing the Horses
and not eating them,
or we are eating the Horses.
We are definitely killing each other.

Speak to me of your appetite.

STEALTHY LIGHT

Someone put the world in our arms.
We are not to ask how to carry it,
nor are we to grow larger for the task,
nor say a word.

This is how the Deer do it,
without fanfare, leaving few signs
of their passage, except
the circle of bent grasses
where they slept last night.

Now, the sun is entering the room,
silently inscribing paisley on the chair back
and engraving the broad trunk
of the eucalyptus where
the bark has fallen away.

We cannot live without
the stealthy light for long.
Caring does not need to announce itself.
Not a square inch of silence
remains on the planet.

We are to shoulder the world quietly
our backs rounding around the burden.
No complaint. No complaint.

SUN FLARE SPEAKS

Sun flare, ice storms and sand storms,
ocean rising up, tsunami,
volcano, rain of fire,
hurricane, child of the melting ice,
tornados, great winds swirling
to revenge Wolves chased by helicopters,
Elephants poached from the air
drowning Polar Bears and irradiated Seals,
Fukushima's lethal wound
upon the Great Mother
and all those birds and animals,
hunted, skinned and brutalized,
and all the trees cut down.

What do we expect
as the good perish
in our mad rush
to death and destruction?

What do we expect,
we who live here,
as if we are
the only ones who matter?

What we war against
grows large to meet us,
spirit protects its own,
life, that is.

What else would we hope for
from the great light
who sees all things?

LABYRINTH

for Waldo

You speak of danger,
and hang extinguishers
as a first act of friendship.
They companion
the water tower
filled to brimming
against a fire storm.

Danger for you,
may be fire,
while for me,
it is probably drought.

The wind is blowing
at 36 miles an hour,
a number in my lexicon
which means *life*, twice,
so once for each of us.
Also referring to
the hidden ones,
the *lamed-vav*
who sustain the world.

Accordingly, you have traced
a labyrinth for us to walk
toward a center
where one asks *the* question.

History says,
the path inward
led to the minotaur.
But history is not certain
whether that animal
was a monster
or a god.

RIFT VALLEY

Between one world and another,
lies the rift and the increasing separation
as the plates of one mind slip away
from the plates of another mind.
I do not question which way I am to go,
but call to my heart to act on the decision made
to follow the soul,
or I will be split apart too,
as so many are,
between violence
and beauty,
between the violent demands of our everyday life,
and the strange beauty of spirit afar.
I must choose beauty,
no matter the cost in this life.
I must choose and leap
across the widening valley;
we cannot rest between.
    Leap!
        Ah Beauty! Receive me in your open arms.

TATTERED FLAGS ACROSS
RICHMOND BRIDGE

for Krystyna

The way two images become one occasion,
because the wind is a messenger,
and, perhaps, also a creator.
Wind, breath, spirit, the same
in languages arising from seeds
carried great distances,
even up river or across the sea
to be planted in distant places.

The land becomes a vast altar
before our eyes as we gaze,
eyes closed, at what is
sanctified between us.
The sacred does not need us
to manufacture anything,
but to tend what springs
from the soil, and even the fire
at the center of the Earth.

Today, an old friend sent a photo:
she is standing in a stream alongside
an Elephant who is healing
from the terrible work of our hands.

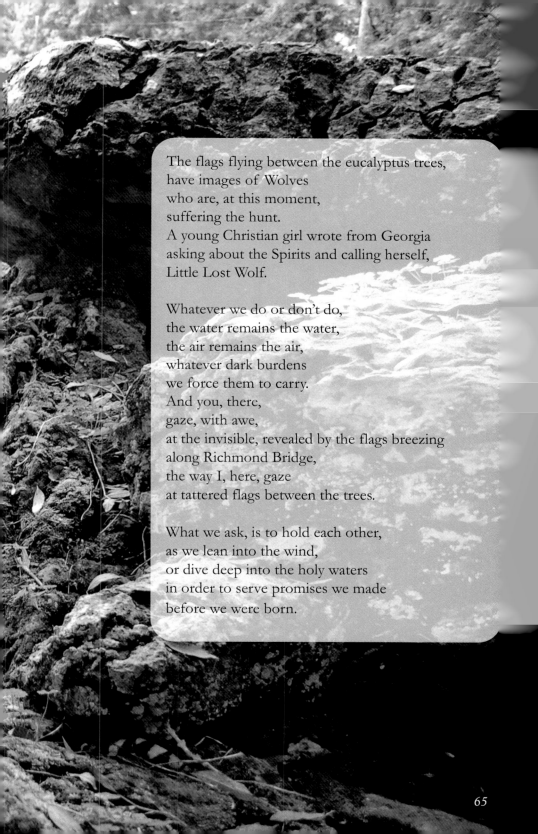

The flags flying between the eucalyptus trees,
have images of Wolves
who are, at this moment,
suffering the hunt.
A young Christian girl wrote from Georgia
asking about the Spirits and calling herself,
Little Lost Wolf.

Whatever we do or don't do,
the water remains the water,
the air remains the air,
whatever dark burdens
we force them to carry.
And you, there,
gaze, with awe,
at the invisible, revealed by the flags breezing
along Richmond Bridge,
the way I, here, gaze
at tattered flags between the trees.

What we ask, is to hold each other,
as we lean into the wind,
or dive deep into the holy waters
in order to serve promises we made
before we were born.

NIGHT CANOE

When the language of prayer
is a tree, walking,
or the steady oars
of a night canoe across the sky,
and each word spoken
is a step on the path
of not gaining on the future,
then, we can also go out,
as we once did,
dodging Spider webs
slung across trees,
trembling
as we give our word.

THE SPIRITS ARE HERE

The spirits are here,
shock and awe,
fear and trembling
in the heart
of fire.

A miniscule white Spider,
the size of a mite,
descends upon these words
and disappears into the
weave of language.

What I do not understand
does not limit beauty,
or deny the constant presence
of the great mystery.

What we have always known,
and what we have forgotten,
is the holy.
Is that we are destroying
the holy.

What we destroy,
sweeps toward us,
an avalanche,
a great flood,
volcano.
We break, we drown,
we burn, are buried
in Earth's trembling.

We could undo our ways.
We could,
so that the prayer
of the small seed
will rise from the earth
like a sunflower.

OUR RADIANT LIVES

Each of us adds to the council of not knowing as our own foaming anguish rises from the radiant sea that is outshining the night sky. "The sacred," was said by someone who studied forgotten and destroyed languages as if they were precious but foreign objects, "...appears when everything is in its place." The sacred assumes place. It assumes you have a place to put your feet and so do I and all other beings. A place that might even be a pillow upon which you lay your head so that you might, tirelessly, watch the moon rainbow across the sky. But if place has disappeared into the wind shear of destruction, has the sacred tumbled down as well into that pit? A poetry of place today as ravaged as the disappeared and out of this partnership, a birth, if any. Repetition follows repetition, radiant, radiant, radiant, like a Rat striking the electrified button to turn on a synapse of relief in a metal cage insuring there is no escape from torture. This does not illuminate how I or you or we could have constructed Fukushima or torture chambers for humans and non-humans. A Rat would not have thought of it, nor the Earth Sea Mother. A mental shift, a brain change, a devolution as rapid and extreme as climate change and caused by the same conditions. We are the Earth, we said, as women concerned that we might disappear into the mindset of the corporate maw, and how you treat us is how you treat the Earth. Or maybe we said the opposite, how you treat the Earth is how you treat us. Or both. Knowledge and understanding are not remedy we came to understand as we stood, and remain, with Cassandra watching the ongoing carnage, as, against our will, we become whores to it. Accepting that people I know have been tortured does not assure me I could survive it or die of it when applied. And science, the great god of a depraved species, will soon offer a procedure or a pill, made of our own DNA, our own genetic material, to wipe out such bitter memories. Other methods tested on veterans suffering PTSD can wipe out the memory of slaughter, what they did, what was done to them, their responsibility or lack of it, so that even wars might be erased from our memory and consciousness will shrivel like an old balloon and the brain wither when it has nothing in it but a false positive of Eden. The soldier forgets that he tortured while his torture victim writhes where she has been dumped to resume her Rat life.

An old memory:

I told a friend, "I can't bear it."
"Who asked you?" she answered.
I thought this was our comedy routine.
She died early, wailing at the injustice of it,
without knowing she was being given the grace
of escaping the rest of the twentieth century
on Planet Earth.

WHEN THE LAST BEAUTY IS ...

Cold rain beat on the brambles. Spirit hiding out
in the brush with the smallest birds. The Squirrels
make a deal with the Sparrows at the feeder,
and the Quail benefit too from the seeds thrown down.

I try to remember what I used to say in the days
when need considered itself supreme.
I could write about loss, disappointment, my body
losing its elasticity or its life, but...
the trash that lines every street in Cairo,
and the black plastic bags
blowing across the Sinai like Ravens ....
You see, I begin thinking only of human concerns,
but I cannot. We have become irrelevant
to the life force, and it is time to remove ourselves
from the center of our own concerns.

I went to the bathroom in the theater,
wiped my ass, my privates, came out and
washed my hands with as little water as possible,
then shook them over the sink. The kind woman asked me
if I wanted a paper towel. "Can't do it anymore," I said.
"The environment?" she asked pleased, I think,
and also startled, as if the basic assumptions
of her life had been axed. "Yes," I said, but I wanted to say,
"Tree, who is my sister, cannot be subsumed in a generality
called the environment. Too many of my kin have died
in the mass graves of language that are holocaust, genocide,
famine and drought."

The first thing you have to know
is that war is entirely personal.
Don't let the helicopter or the AK47 fool you.

The Wolf running until his lungs burst
to escape aerial slaughter,
likewise, the Elephant, also the human child
racing to outrun a drone,
knows his or her death violates every cosmic law,
and still that doesn't save them.
God exists and is heartbroken.
That is why you hear lament in every niche
where beauty still resides.
When the last beauty is exterminated
by the madmen we so adore
that we pay them with our life's blood,
then God will proclaim
a funeral for the world and bellow pain through eternity.

How can I know what God prefers —
to be alone forever with the ashes of creation,
or to watch it go down again and again and again.
One way or another, even the Divine
cannot escape the infinity of what we destroy.
I look at my wet hands. Water. A single drop.
     Who, among us, could imagine it?

FIRE AND FIRE AND FIRE

Red-headed Woodpecker,
knocking at the dying elm,
a flurry of Finches, red and golden
against the flaming sky.

It's simple.
Tell it again and again:
It's over!
Unless there's a miracle
of our own making.

I pour water for the Bees
who cling, thirstily,
to the wet stone,
drink without drowning,
then fly away
to seize honey from the pepper trees.

Birds and Squirrels come to another bowl
and another for Rabbits, Coyotes,
unknown who else
gathers around Her
in her decline.

It is cooler here among the trees.

God wants a home
like every other creature
not an eviction notice
or a fire sale.

The heat intensifies.
Light becomes fire.
God's fevered brow.

This patio,
a hospice, a bedside vigil,
that might,
if we ever learn a true medicine,
restore the only life
that matters at this time.

FOR NAOMI

These
cracked vessels
hold
water.

A GREATER SILENCE

Soon, there will be
a greater silence
than there is now.

I do not want
to be here
alone.

When the last tree falls
may I be under it.
May the last tree
    take me down.

About the Author

Deena Metzger is a writer and healer living at the end of the road in Topanga, California. Her books include the novels *A Rain of Night Birds, La Negra y Blanca,* (winner of the 2012 Oakland Pen Award); *Feral; Doors: A Fiction for Jazz Horn; The Other Hand; What Dinah Thought; Skin: Shadows/Silence, A Love Letter in the Form of a Novel* and *The Woman Who Slept With Men to Take the War Out of Them* – a novel in the form of a play. The latter is included in *Tree: Essays and Pieces,* which features her celebrated Warrior Poster on its cover testifying to a woman's triumph over breast cancer.

Her books of poetry include, *Ruin and Beauty: New and Collected Poems, A Sabbath Among The Ruins, Looking for the Faces of God, The Axis Mundi Poems* and *Dark Milk.*

Writing For Your Life: A Guide and Companion to the Inner Worlds is her classic text on writing and the imagination. Two plays *Not As Sleepwalkers* and *Dreams Against the State* have been produced in theaters and various venues. She co-edited the anthology, *Intimate Nature: The Bond Between Women and Animals,* one of the first testimonies to the reality and nature of animal intelligence and agency. *Entering the Ghost River: Meditations on the Theory and Practice of Healing,* and *From Grief Into Vision: A Council* examine the tragic failure of contemporary culture and provide guidance for personal, political, environmental and spiritual healing.

Deena is a radical thinker on behalf of the natural world and planetary survival, a teacher of writing and healing practices for 50 years and a writer and activist profoundly concerned with peacemaking, restoration and sanctuary for a beleaguered world. She has been convening ReVisioning Medicine – bringing Indigenous medicine ways to heal the medical world – since 2004, and is imagining a Literature of Restoration as foundations of a new viable culture. She, with writer Michael Ortiz Hill, introduced Daré to North America in 1999. Daré and the 19 Ways Training for the 5th World, are unique forms of individual, community and environmental healing based on Indigenous and contemporary medicine and wisdom traditions.